The YES Book for Teenagers

By

Susan Louise Peterson

All rights reserved © 2013 by Susan Louise Peterson

No part of this book may be reproduced or transmitted in any form or by any means, graphic, electronic, or mechanical, including photocopying, recording, taping, or by any information storage retrieval system, without the written permission of the publisher.

For information address:

Vilnius Press

244 Fifth Avenue

New York, NY 10001

Printed in the United States of America

CONTENTS

Foreword	ii
Preface	v
Acknowledgements	vi
Introduction	vii
Chapter 1 Yes Could Mean That More Review is Needed	1
Chapter 2 Yes Could Mean You Need	12
Chapter 3 Yes Could Mean There are Communication Difficulties	23
Chapter 4 Yes Could Involve a Need to Increase Social Interaction	34
Chapter 5 Yes Could Mean You are Making Transitions	45
Chapter 6 Yes Could Mean You are on a Learning Cycle	56
Chapter 7 Yes Could Mean to Think of Your Relation to Others	67
Chapter 8 Yes Could Mean Implementing New Ideas	78
Chapter 9 Yes Could Mean Life Changes are Happening	89
Recommended Reading for Teenagers	100
Index	101
About the Author	106

FOREWORD

The Yes Book for Teenagers is a book that encourages better communication and understanding between parents and teens, a perspective of what 'yes' could mean. I know **that** seems confusing because 'yes' means 'yes' and parents probably say 'no or maybe' more so than 'yes.' However, when parents, coaches, teachers or other authority figures say 'yes' before "jumping the gun" it's important to understand the scope of their answer and all aspects as it relates to you, others and the particular situation.

The first thing that came to mind when I read this book is in communication with my Olympic Speed Skating Coach. We (the USA team) are sent a workout via e-mail in the beginning of the week. However, there's always the chance that my coach could adjust the scheduled workout at anytime. As an athlete it's my responsibility to make sure I'm not missing important training and that my body and mind are both prepared for the workout on the schedule. I need to show up with the proper sleep, enough water for the workout and wearing the right clothes. If we complete a workout before the set time of our usual session, I will ask the coach if we are finished with the workout. If he wants me to skate extra, he will encourage me to practice my on ice skills until the time has run out. However, if he says 'yes' and allows me to get off the ice he means 'yes-but' we may have more off ice training to complete and for sure need to cool down from the workout. So, although we are technically finished with the main on ice workout that doesn't mean that I can leave and go home to sleep in my bed or talk on the phone. It means there is more work to do!

The Yes Book for Teenagers challenges your thought process and helps in this basic but often miscommunication.

> **Allison Baver**
> 2010 Olympic Bronze Medalist, Short Track Speed Skater
> "I need to show up with a winning attitude."

PREFACE

As a mother of teenage twin daughters and a school psychologist I realize that 'yes' can have multiple meanings. Sometimes as a parent, I say 'yes' to my teenage children for their numerous requests. Later, I realize that I really needed to explain what is meant with a little more detail. My 'yes' response to their questions and requests could have really meant that I actually needed to provide them with more information to think about in making their personal choices.

As I observe teenagers on a daily basis I see that they often make 'fast and quick' requests because they want to go with friends or do an activity at a moment's notice. Some requests are thought out by the teenager, but other requests are 'off the cuff' and little thought is considered because of the rapid pace of the teenager's life. This book is written to help teenagers see the broad considerations of a 'yes' response by their parents and other adults in their lives. It is hoped that teenagers and the adults that work with them can see the broader meaning of a simple 'yes' response.

ACKNOWLEDGEMENTS

I am grateful to the many people who have influenced my writing career. For a writer, a simple idea or comment that someone shares with you can inspire an article or a book. The many education professionals, school psychologists and students in the public school have been a writing inspiration to me. I certainly want to thank my husband and twin daughters for putting up with a writer's crazy schedule and for being supportive on my journey to express myself through the printed word. A big thanks to Vilnius Press who always goes the extra mile to make the publishing experience pleasant.

I would like to thank Nick Johnson, a national Yo Yo competitor and Austin Wierschke, the two time U.S. National Texting Champion for their kind words on the book. I would also like to thank David Kelly, the 2012 National President of HOSA-Future Health Professionals for his professional attitude and the strong leader example he provides to his organization and teenagers around the country. I would also like to express my appreciation to Allison Baver, an Olympic speed skater for her contribution in writing the foreword for the book.

INTRODUCTION

Teenagers are usually requesting something from their parents, teachers or other adults in their lives. The adults' responses to the requests are varied, but often a 'yes' response indicates that there are still some things to think about in relation to the request. As a teenager, you are on a mission in life and part of that mission is learning to understand how a 'yes' response can impact your life.

For example, a 'yes' response could mean that more review is needed for the request or that you are not really looking at the big picture. The 'yes' from your parents may be a call that there are communication difficulties or that you are seeing yourself in relation to others as you learn to increase social interaction. Basically, the 'yes' response from parents and other adults helps you on your path of making transitions and implementing new ideas. The big picture for you is that as a teenager you are definitely on a learning cycle and that life changes are happening at a rapid pace in your life.

CHAPTER ONE
Yes could mean more review is needed

Although, you are told 'yes' to your request, it could mean that more review is needed. Your parent may be telling you that additional questions need to be answered or reconsidered. There may be a need for you to check the details or prepare more information for your request.

Sometimes teachers and parents want you to think about your actions before you go with your request. The adults may want you to re-evaluate your idea or have you reconvene before the request is approved. Yes might mean the request is not approved yet and there are additional steps such as additional information or modifying your request before the final approval.

Yes might mean more things need to be reconsidered

"Yes, the council is being formed, but did you pick a diverse group of students on the council?"

"Yes, Billy is a good choice for the club president, but did you discuss the time commitment with him?"

"Yes, you would be a great nominee, but are you sure you want to do this?"

"Yes, you can certainly participate in the food drive, but did you discuss it with your parents?"

"Yes, the teen board is considering your application, but would you consider a different position on the board?"

Yes might mean that questions need to be answered

"Yes, the paper is long enough, but did you add the summary?"

"Yes, the poster board is finished, but where is the conclusion section?"

"Yes, the computer project is coming along, but where are the graphs and how are you going to use them in the project?"

"Yes, your rehearsal was nice, but did all of the students in your group audition and have a part in the play?"

"Yes, your paper met the deadline, but what is the purpose of your paper?"

☙

Yes might mean you are not totally prepared

"Yes, your report is finished, but did you take a copy of the report and turn it into the teacher?"

"Yes, your power point presentation is complete, but did you save it on your flash drive?"

"Yes, your speech is done, but have you practiced saying it out loud?"

"Yes, your team has practiced, but did you all discuss your strategy for the game on Friday?"

"Yes, you had the play rehearsal, but did you check to see if the costumes and props were ready for the performance?"

Yes might mean there are some details that need to be checked

"Yes, the flight reservations are made, but did you check the airport luggage weight limits?"

"Yes, the camp registration is completed, but did you get driving directions to the camp?"

"Yes, your team is almost ready to pack the van, but did you conduct an equipment check before you load it?"

"Yes, we can go to the swim meet, but did you pack the towels and goggles?"

"Yes, the party is almost ready, but did you check to see if there are enough drinks in the refrigerator?"

Yes might mean you need to review something

"Yes, your term paper is complete, but did you proof it for mistakes?"

"Yes, your team project is done, but did you decide who is doing each part of the presentation?"

"Yes, your art project is finished, but did you find a box to put it in for transportation to school?"

"Yes, your take home test is completed, but did you check it for math errors?"

"Yes, the cake is baked, but do you have all of the cake decorating supplies?"

ଔ

Yes might mean you need to think about your actions

"Yes, you can go without her, but think about how she will feel if you don't invite her and she sees you with all of your friends?"

"Yes, you can do back to class, but it would be thoughtful if you apologize to your teacher."

"Yes, you can have a soda in the front yard, but think about where you put the empty can."

"Yes, you can paint in your room, but think about the cleanup."

"Yes, you can go on the trip, but think about how tired you will be when you return from the trip."

Yes might mean you need to re-evaluate your position

"Yes, you can be the team captain, but are you comfortable directing other team members?"

"Yes, you have an edge over the other team, but have you thought about how much experience they are bringing to the game?"

"Yes, you have a long time until the regional competition, but have you considered how much preparation is needed before you get there?"

"Yes, you can skip the rehearsal, but have you thought about how it will impact the other actors in the play?"

"Yes, you can be on the speech team, but you also need to write and practice your speech before the contest."

Yes might mean it is necessary to reconvene

"Yes, you passed the true/false test, but did you meet with your instructor about your written responses?"

"Yes, you explained the incident to the teacher, but you have to defend your actions to the Dean."

"Yes, the event proposal has been accepted by the student council, but it has to be presented to the principal."

"Yes, the request was approved, but you must present an itemized list of the costs to the school treasurer."

"Yes, you can participate on the sports team, but you must sign a behavioral agreement before the first game."

☙

Yes might mean the request is not approved yet

"Yes, the trip to the state conference is planned, but we will have to raise enough funds to get the final approval for the trip."

"Yes, the fall dance plans are made, but the principal has to approve our ideas."

"Yes, the teacher has the recommendation form, but she has to send it before you are accepted in the camp."

"Yes, you can apply for engineering camp, but you are not approved until you mail an official transcript."

"Yes, the school newspaper article is complete, but it needs to be approved by the editorial board."

Yes might mean you need to modify your request

"Yes, you can be on a cheerleading squad, but you have to commit to cheerleading practice two days a week."

"Yes, your application is tentatively approved, but you have to add your goals before you get final approval."

"Yes, you have the job, but first you have to agree to wear a uniform to work."

"Yes, you can go on the trip, but you will have to bring back the parent permission slip before we leave."

"Yes, your essay was fine, but you need to expand your ideas to raise your grade."

ஐ

CHAPTER TWO
Yes could mean you need to look at the "big picture"

When adults tell you 'yes' they could be saying that you need to look at the big picture. This could be a hint you are only looking at part of the information or have completed half of the steps in the process. Sometimes your request may lack focus and goes in many different directions. At other times, you may be only focused on one thing.

There could be more to the story, more people involved in the situation or that the situation involves greater involvement by you. Teachers and adults may help warn you of setbacks in your plan. Parents may be helping you to retrace your steps and just want you to think about the consequences of your request.

Yes might mean you have only part of the information

"Yes, you can take the class, but call the instructor to discuss the specific requirements for the class."

"Yes, you can go to the movies, but check the start and end times."

"Yes, you can enroll in the camp, but check the pickup and drop off locations."

"Yes, you can join the soccer club, but find out the cost of the uniform."

"Yes, you are allowed on the swim team, but first you need to check the morning practice schedule."

ଔ

Yes might mean there is more to the story

"Yes, you can go with Beth, but have you told your plans to her parents?"

"Yes, you can go to a birthday party, but only if his parents are the chaperones."

"Yes, you are allowed in the museum, but only if an adult accompanies the group."

"Yes, you are planning a celebration, but have you contacted the school about permission to use the gym."

"Yes, you hope the meeting works out, but have you made plans to have security for a large group."

ଓ

Yes might mean there are more people involved in the situation

"Yes, you told your teacher your idea, but did you run it by your group leader?"

"Yes, you're designing the power point, but are you consulting with other team members?"

"Yes, you have worked hard on the project, but did you divide the work evenly between the group members?"

"Yes, you can plan a field trip, but have you contacted the hospital tour guides about the date?"

Yes, you can attend the conference, but you have to organize a team to be selected for the competition."

ଔ

Yes might mean you have completed only half the steps

"Yes, you submitted the application, but did you ask the teacher to fill out the recommendation form?"

"Yes, you wrote the paper, but did you proof it for errors and corrections?"

"Yes, you can join the health career club, but did you pay your dues for the school year?"

"Yes, you are allowed to perform, but have you submitted the grade check form to your advisor before the performance?"

"Yes, you can apply to the program, but the 15 page application needs to be completed by Saturday."

☙

Yes might mean there could be a setback in your plans

"Yes, you can go to the game, but transportation is an issue."

"Yes, you can attend the concert, but you have to pay for the ticket yourself."

"Yes, you are invited to the club, but you need passing grades to join the club."

"Yes, the performance is Saturday, but you have a very long drive and will be returning late from the school trip."

"Yes, you can go to the play, but you need to check your work schedule first."

Yes might mean you are focused on one thing

"Yes, you completed your term paper, but did you finish the rest of the English writing assignments?"

"Yes, you studied your Algebra final, but did you study for the finals in your other 4 classes?"

"Yes, the art project is complete, but did you finish your art supply list?"

"Yes, your essay is excellent, but did you cite the references?"

"Yes, your practice performance has been good, but did you watch the strategy tapes for more ideas?"

ಬ

Yes might mean the project requires greater involvement

"Yes, you can participate in field day, but it requires that you volunteer for two hours."

"Yes, you can attend the conference, but each high school must present a poster presentation."

"Yes, you can compete in the state swim competion, but it requires travel out of town to the meet."

"Yes, you can go to the teen leadership conference, but you have to work in the booth for a half day."

"Yes, you can work toward the gold award, but it requires a big commitment to complete community service activities."

Yes might mean the request needs a focus

"Yes, your paper is neat enough, but what is the focus of your paper?"

"Yes, your team can go to the track meet, but you all need to decide what events each person will compete in."

"Yes, you can run for state officer, but what is the platform of your campaign?"

"Yes, you can be in the pageant, but what talent will you showcase?"

"Yes, you can run for student government, but you need to make posters for your campaign."

ଓ

Yes might mean you need to retrace your steps

"Yes, you can prepare the graduation speech, but you need to think about all of the teachers and staff who helped you."

"Yes, you can go on another trip to Jennifer's house, but you need to map out directions since you lost your way last week."

"Yes, you lost your purse, but think about all of the places you visited yesterday."

"Yes, you misplaced your cell phone, but have your sister call it and see if it rings."

"Yes, the textbook is missing, but have you checked your closet and looked around your bedroom?"

☙

Yes might mean think about the consequences

"Yes, you can go with your new friend, but think about how your best friend will feel."

"Yes, you can walk on the beach, but do you think it's safe to go far away from the group leader?"

"Yes, you can go to the party, but how much do you know about the person who invited you?"

"Yes, you can ride with your friends, but think about how many people are crammed in the car."

"Yes, you can take the bus, but check to see if the drop off schedule will get you to practice in time."

CHAPTER THREE

Yes could mean there are communication difficulties

A 'yes' response by adults can mean they are helping you to sort out communication difficulties. Perhaps they are allowing you to consider how you are annoying others or disrupting others with your actions. At other times, you may be complaining too much, not paying attention, avoiding others, taking things too seriously and are getting too easily upset. The communication difficulties may also be one sided. The adult might be telling you to listen more closely or to be clear with your responses to others.

Yes might mean you are avoiding other people

"Yes, you can go to the beach, but don't go off by yourself."

"Yes, you can go to the camp, but it is very important to always stay with a buddy in the outdoors."

"Yes, you can go to a big convention, but stay with the group of kids from your school."

"Yes, you can do the project, but you need a partner to bounce off your ideas."

"Yes, you are allowed on the team, but you can't practice alone as you need to be part of the team practice."

Yes might mean you are annoying to others

"Yes, you can have a party, but keep the noise level down as the walls in this house are very thin."

"Yes, you can go to the workshop, but slow down so you don't run into other people."

"Yes, you can have a cell phone, but turn it off during class time."

"Yes, you can listen to the radio, but turn it down so it doesn't bother the class next door."

"Yes, you can have food at the party, but pick up the trash and don't leave a mess in the classroom."

☙

Yes might mean things look one-sided

"Yes, you can watch your television show first, but the next time it is your sister's turn to pick her program."

"Yes, you can pick your desert first, but remember your friends may want the same desert you choose."

"Yes, you want to go, but did you think about how your brother will feel about staying home."

"Yes, you can go to the other school, but won't you miss spending time with your friends?"

"Yes, you can join the new team, but it leaves one less player on the main team."

ଛ

Yes might mean you are not paying attention

"Yes, you can walk to the store, but pay attention to the traffic at the crosswalks."

"Yes, you can take the exam early, but pay attention to the bells so you know when to finish the exam."

"Yes, you can take the class with your friends, but listen closely to the teacher."

"Yes, you can be in the group project, but listen carefully to the directions from the group leader."

"Yes, you can be a life guard, but play close attention to everything that goes on in the pool."

ଓ

Yes might mean you need to have awareness of others

"Yes, you can go to the all school conference, but be aware of the different school zones so you can find the bus."

"Yes, you are able to go to the rodeo, but sit near people you know."

"Yes, you can be in the play, but you need to respect each other's part in the play."

"Yes, you can be on the team, but remember each player has a different position."

"Yes, you are allowed to go to afterschool clubs, but stay in the assigned classroom."

Yes might mean you are complaining too much

"Yes, you can ride with the neighbors, but don't complain about the size of their car."

"Yes, you can join the cheerleading squad, but don't be so critical of the team leader."

"Yes, you can talk about your teacher, but don't challenge everything he does."

"Yes, you are allowed on the team, but don't have so many disagreements with the team sponsor."

"Yes, you can be part of the regional drama team, but don't be so demanding about your costume."

Yes might mean you are too easily upset

"Yes, you can go to camp, but don't get upset when we drive away."

"Yes, you can go to the party, but don't let a little teasing upset you so much."

"Yes, you are allowed to participate in the state contest, but don't let the big crowds and large number of people upset you."

"Yes, you can travel to the fair, but don't get upset by the long distance."

"Yes, you can go to the dance, but don't get upset if someone laughs at your dancing."

Yes might mean you need to listen more closely

"Yes, you can go to the lecture, but listen to the main points."

"Yes, you can talk with your friend about the wreck, but listen as she talks about her struggles."

"Yes, you may go to the performance, but listen for key lines in the play."

"Yes, you can hear the class presentations, but listen as your classmates make their presentations."

"Yes, you can go to the poster presentation, but listen as the teams present their research."

☙

Yes might mean you are disrupting others with your actions

"Yes, you can camp out, but don't invade the other camper's space."

"Yes, you can go to the jamboree, but don't litter the campground."

"Yes, you can go to the seminar, but don't text when the presenter is speaking."

"Yes, you are allowed in the theatre, but all cell phones must be turned off."

"Yes, you may go to the party, but be very quiet and don't disturb your father as he is sleeping and needs his rest."

ଌ

Yes might mean your responses are unclear

"Yes, you answered the phone, but did you tell him that we are running late?"

"Yes, you told the neighbors we were out of town, but did you let them know we will be back on Saturday?"

"Yes, you told your teacher about the accident, but did you let her know you will have many doctor's appointments?"

"Yes, you can go to the competition, but did you tell your teacher you will be out Friday?"

"Yes, you can attend the weekly internship, but did you clarify the details with your counselor?"

☙

CHAPTER FOUR
Yes could mean a need to increase social interaction

Adults may use a 'yes' responses to help you focus on your social interactions with others. The parent could want you to give feedback, to provide an example or to be a good example for others. Social interaction can be as simple as making introductions to others and providing open communication. Social interaction requests may also involve providing support to someone else and talking about feelings to others. It may include admitting a mistake to someone or having a conversation about an issue. The 'yes' response can also have the intention to share your interests with others. It may also be a way to share talents and find out about the talents of others.

Yes might mean you need to make introductions

"Yes, you can have a party at the house, but you need to introduce me to the guests."

"Yes, you can go to the job interview, but first introduce yourself to the staff."

"Yes, the coach is interested in recruiting you, but you have to introduce yourself to the team."

"Yes, you can go to the installation, but you will need to make a formal introduction at the ball."

"Yes, you can volunteer at the hospital, but first introduce yourself to the volunteer coordinator."

☙

Yes might mean you need to provide support to someone

"Yes, you can go to the mall, but listen to Laura's concerns."

"Yes, you can invite John over, but let him share his struggles with you."

"Yes, you can spend the day with Mark, but give him a listening ear."

"Yes, you can attend the club meeting with Jill, but remember she just lost her grandfather and may need to talk about it."

"Yes, you can visit Sonny, but think about how he is feeling since his mother lost her job over a year ago."

Yes might mean you need to provide an example

"Yes, you can give the directions to the class, but first show them how to use the computer map system."

"Yes, you can conduct the experiment, but first demonstrate each step."

"Yes, you can instruct the girls on how to model, but first show them how to make a turn on the ramp."

"Yes, you can show the kids your new dance, but first teach them the steps of the dance."

"Yes, you can lead the cheer, but first give an example of the movements."

Yes might mean you need to give feedback

"Yes, you can attend the talk, but your teacher wants you to answer feedback questions."

"Yes, you can go on the mystery shopping trip, but you have to account for the way you were treated as a customer."

"Yes, you can go to the conference, but you have to complete the feedback survey."

"Yes, you can be involved in planning the conference, but you have to give feedback on how to improve it next year."

"Yes, you can consult with the students, but you have to give them a chance to share their feelings."

Yes might mean you need to talk about your feelings

"Yes, you can visit your friend, but you need to talk about what happened last Friday."

"Yes, you can see Joe, but you should talk to him about the money you loaned him."

"Yes, you can see your Dad, but talk with him about your struggles with the divorce."

"Yes, you can talk with the school counselor, but tell her about your stress with the class load."

"Yes, you can visit with the Dean, but explain your side of the situation."

ଚ

Yes might mean you need to admit a mistake to someone

"Yes, you can go to the library, but apologize to the librarian for dropping the book in the mud."

"Yes, you can see your friend on Friday, but tell her you are sorry for missing her birthday party."

"Yes, you can join the drama club again, but apologize for skipping the meetings last year."

"Yes, you can go to the job fair, but apologize to the representative for missing the job interview."

"Yes, you can be on the drill team, but apologize for missing the practice on Saturday."

Yes might mean you need to have a conversation with someone

"Yes, you can go, but talk about your project with Beth."

"Yes, you can audition, but talk with the director about your music selection."

"Yes, you are allowed to participate in the regional competition, but talk with the drama coach about the requirements."

"Yes, there is a game on Friday, but talk with your doctor and get the medical clearance."

"Yes, there is a test on Saturday, but ask the counselor how to register for it."

☙

Yes might mean you need to model a good example for others

"Yes, the game is this week, but model good game behavior for the other team as they have difficulty in that area."

"Yes, he fouled you, but be a good sport about it."

"Yes, she hit you, but don't retaliate or strike back at her."

"Yes, the boy yelled at you, but stay calm even when he is upset."

"Yes, your friend was unfair in eating the whole pizza, but be a good sport and next time show him you take only one or two pieces."

ಬ

Yes might mean you need to share your talents with others

"Yes, you can dance well, but share your skills with your Physical Education teacher."

"Yes, you have a unique talent in archery so you may want to enter the local contest."

"Yes, you really sing well, but it would be nice to share your talent in the school choir."

"Yes, your project shows a lot of color and detail, so you might want to take the advanced design class next year."

"Yes, your drama performance was excellent, so you might want to participate in the talent showcase in May."

Yes might mean you need to share your interests with others

"Yes, you have a unique skill in quilting and you may want to join a quilting club."

"Yes, your knowledge about ping pong rules is very strong, so you might want to take the ping pong referee class."

"Yes, your skill on the balance beam is promising so you may want to take a class to perfect your technique."

"Yes, you enjoy public speaking, so you may want to go to the speaking forum on Tuesday."

"Yes, you like horses so much, you might enjoy volunteering at the horse farms on weekends."

CHAPTER FIVE
Yes could mean you are making transitions

Yes could mean that parents and adults are helping you to make transitions in life. On a positive note, they can help you to develop better habits. The adults may be assisting you as you take a practical approach in life. This might include focusing on your personal decisions.

The transition may be focused on having you examine your strengths and weaknesses. This allows you to realize your limitations and find trouble spots in your plan. Parents and adults are helping you to be more adaptive in this changing world. These adults are here for you when you need a supportive environment.

Yes might mean you are making a transition

"Yes, you can go to the job fair, but explore the different types of part time jobs."

"Yes, you can be part of the conference, but you might want to volunteer to facilitate a poster session."

"Yes, you are allowed to attend the seminar, but you should really collect the career brochures."

"Yes, many colleges are offering scholarships, but you need to check out your best scholarship options."

"Yes, you can be on the dance team, but you need to create your own individual dance performance."

Yes might mean you are examining your weaknesses

"Yes, you can type, but that is not your strongest area."

"Yes, you can sing in the choir, but you need some additional training to strengthen your voice."

"Yes, you can take gymnastics, but you really have upper body strength more suited for the volleyball team."

"Yes, you are allowed to compete in the butterfly stroke final, but the breast stroke is your stronger event."

"Yes, you definitely have potential in playing basketball, but your natural abilities are stronger in baseball."

☙

Yes might mean you are focused on your strengths

"Yes, your paper is well written and shows your strength in writing composition."

"Yes, your presentation was well organized and clearly shows your skills in organizing materials."

"Yes, your speech was presented well and it was clear you are an excellent public speaker."

"Yes, your demonstration earned an A because you thought out each step of the demonstration."

"Yes, your poster was very creative and it was clear that you have excellent artistic abilities."

Yes might mean you realize you may have some limitations

"Yes, you can take the course, but you have a transportation limitation on how to get to class."

"Yes, you can write a book on surfing, but you may be short of time to complete it this year."

"Yes, you can have a party, but you are limited to inviting ten friends."

"Yes, you can join motorcycle racing, but you will need additional money for the racing uniform and helmet."

"Yes, you can be on the elite dance team, but you will need additional funds for lessons from a specialized coach."

ಬ

Yes might mean you understand there are trouble spots

"Yes, you can go to New York for the contest, but the airport is announcing weather delays."

"Yes, you qualify for the modeling competition, but there is a possibility the contest could be cancelled because of a low number of entries."

"Yes, the team finals are scheduled in September, but there have been some changes in the coaches so the practice time may change."

"Yes, you are an alternate for the team, but it is uncertain if you will play in the finals."

"Yes, you can go to the state conference, but you will have to make up homework."

Yes might mean you are developing better habits

"Yes, you can stay up until 11:00 p.m. tonight because you took a nap earlier today."

"Yes, you can eat pizza for dinner, because you had a healthy lunch."

"Yes, you can drive to the store because you have been being careful with the car."

"Yes, you can go out to the pool at Mike's because you have been good about wearing sunscreen."

"Yes, you can let your hair grow out long, because you have been trimming it on a regular basis."

Yes might mean you need to find a supportive environment

"Yes, you have a lot of friends, but you need to find more reliable friends."

"Yes, your friend could take you, but is she dependable so that you arrive on time?"

"Yes, the group has many kids, but do the kids get along well enough to complete the project?"

"Yes, you really like Kelly and Jill, but do they share the same interest in completing high school as you do?"

"Yes, you can have a lot of friends, but you need to think about how they fit into your future plans."

Yes might mean you need to be more adaptive

"Yes, you can go to the magnet high school, but you have to choose a different major, since your major selection was full."

"Yes, you can go to camp, but you have to go to a different location than the one your selected."

"Yes, you can be on a team, but you have to be willing to be on the team that picks you."

"Yes, you go to the seminar, but you have to be flexible on attending the day or night session."

"Yes, you can go to the tennis tournament, but check the schedule and be aware that the schedule can change at a moment's notice."

☙

Yes might mean you need to take a practical approach

"Yes, you can read the speech word for word, but try to make it sound more natural."

"Yes, you can memorize the answers from the book, but try to apply the information to realistic situations."

"Yes, you can travel straight from the conference, but you might want to stop and rest since it is a long trip."

"Yes, you could try to complete all the projects in one night, but it is not practical as you will be exhausted."

"Yes, you can take two hard courses, but it seems more practical to take a hard course with an easy course to avoid too much homework."

Yes might mean you are making a personal decision

"Yes, you can go to the seminar, but you need to decide which sessions you want to take."

"Yes, you can have a new dress for the prom, but you need to decide what color suits you best."

"Yes, you can attend the junior college next year, but you need to pick a major from the college catalog."

"Yes, you can pick out a car, but it has to be in the lower price range."

"Yes, you can buy a class ring, but think about the style you want to select."

ଓ

CHAPTER SIX
Yes could mean you are on a learning Cycle

Parents and adults are helping you to see life as one big learning cycle. They are helping you learn to handle disagreements. This includes watching you learn to react to new situations. There will also be many opportunities for you to learn and make life observations. You will be on a path to get a realistic view of the world and understand the world as a complex place. You will learn there are problems to solve. There may be times when you are learning to collaborate with others. However, learning can come full cycle when you learn to value differences in people.

Yes might mean you are establishing a routine

"Yes, you can go to town, but decide where you want to go first."

"Yes, you can drive to school, but decide the easiest route to take to school."

"Yes, you have a class schedule, but make a list of the classroom numbers so you know where to go."

"Yes, your first day of school is tomorrow, but lay out your clothes so you can decide what to wear."

"Yes, you have a backpack, but organize your notebooks for each class."

Yes might mean you are learning to handle disagreements

"Yes, you can go with your friends, but don't get in the middle of their argument."

"Yes, you can disagree with your teacher, but remember you should still respect her position."

"Yes, you can take a stand with your position, but you still need to cooperate with the players on the team."

"Yes, you can present your point of view, but try to be sensitive to other people's view point."

"Yes, you can argue your point, but consider that others might not agree with you."

Yes might mean you are learning to react to situations

"Yes, you can volunteer at the hospital, but be aware that many people are struggling with health issues."

"Yes, you can invite your friend, but understand she is sad about her parent's divorce."

"Yes, you can help your teacher, but be aware that she had surgery and can't lift heavy items."

"Yes, you can go to the game, but realize there is a lot of tension between the opposing teams."

"Yes, you can go to the dance, but you won't know most of the people since you are not from that school."

Yes might mean you are making life observations

"Yes, you can go to the movie, but check the movie ratings."

"Yes, you can go on the senior trip, but make sure you are on the right bus when you return."

"Yes, you can participate in the state finals, but go to the exhibit hall and check out the colleges represented."

"Yes, you can consider joining the military, but talk to some of the soldiers before you sign any papers."

"Yes, you can go with your friends, but think about what type of people they are and their beliefs."

Yes might mean you are getting a realistic view

"Yes, you were assigned a group project, so have you consulted with the group members?"

"Yes, you are going on your first plane trip, but have you checked your flight plans and printed up your boarding passes?"

"Yes, you lost the last game, but you need to think about what game strategy you want to use next."

"Yes, the competition was tough, but you fared well against top performers."

"Yes, we did not place in the regional finals, but we learned many things we want to do different next year."

☙

Yes might mean you are learning that life is complex

"Yes, you can attend the seminar, but you must first complete the registration packet."

"Yes, you can go to the class, but you have to submit official transcripts before you can attend."

"Yes, you can take the test, but you will have to pay a late registration fee."

"Yes, you can take the class, but you will have to wait until second semester to enroll in it."

"Yes, you were hurt and can't compete in this game, but you will heal and things will get better."

Yes might mean you are learning to collaborate with others

"Yes, you can attend the show, but work out the details with your teacher."

"Yes, the group is presenting tomorrow, but your group members need to practice the presentation."

"Yes, the coach is allowing the team to practice, but check with his assistant for details."

"Yes, you can rehearse tonight, but get permission from the custodian to unlock the room."

"Yes, your team is almost ready, but you need to discuss who is playing the different roles."

Yes might mean you are learning to value differences

"Yes, you can join the club, but realize everyone is different."

"Yes, the trip overseas will be valuable and introduce you to a new culture."

"Yes, the purpose of the multicultural club is to introduce you to many cultures."

"Yes, you are different from Juan, but you should still respect each other."

"Yes, there is a major disagreement between the clubs, but we still need to work together on the float."

Yes might mean you are learning to problem solve

"Yes, your group is not on the same page about the project, but you can still work out a solution to the problem."

"Yes, you have a big problem, but you can talk to the teacher about your next step."

"Yes, one group member dropped out, but you can still discuss who will take over her responsibilities."

"Yes, you all can go on the trip, but you can't get a bus for that day so you will have to change the trip date."

"Yes, you can have the dance, but you will need to work out the food arrangements."

ಬ

Yes might mean that life is full of connections

"Yes, you are against the other team, but remember you might play together in a regional game."

"Yes, you don't care for his personality, but you still attend class together at school."

"Yes, you have issues with her, but you will see her at school and church."

"Yes, your teacher is difficult, but don't forget that it is a small school and you will probably have him again next year."

"Yes, he gets on your nerves, but he is still your neighbor."

ଔ

CHAPTER SEVEN

Yes could mean to think about your relation to others

A 'yes' response can be telling you to think about your personal self and then expand your relationship with others. For instance, you can respond to a 'yes' by thinking about your personal health and how you might sequence events in your life. You can be learning how to state your own opinion and making new discoveries about yourself. You will then learn to step outside yourself and think if you are misleading others or losing your credibility with others. There could also be suspicious circumstances related to your request. Yes could be a caution not to isolate yourself from others. Most importantly, a yes response can be used to help build trust with others.

Yes might mean you need to think about improving your health

"Yes, you can go hiking, but if you don't drink enough water you will dehydrate."

"Yes, you can go to school without breakfast, but how are you going to feel in a few hours?"

"Yes, you can walk to school with your friends, but are you going to wear high heels or walking shoes?"

"Yes, you can go up in the mountains, but pack a first aid kit in your backpack."

"Yes, you can wear heels to the dance, but be careful because it is easy to sprain an ankle."

Yes might mean you need to sequence events

"Yes, your make up looks good, but are you going to eat breakfast before you leave for school?"

"Yes, your homework is complete, but did you organize it in your backpack?"

"Yes, you finished your artwork, but did you put it in your art portfolio?"

"Yes, the World History project looks great, but shouldn't you box it up before you take it to school?"

"Yes, the Geometry test is Friday, but did you make plans to study Thursday night?"

Yes might mean you need to step outside yourself

"Yes, you can be part of that group of friends, but realize your other friends may be hurt by your decision."

"Yes, it is totally your right to do what you want, but is it really being respectful to your teacher?"

"Yes, you can make your own decision, but think about the impact it will have on your friendships."

"Yes, you can change teams, but are you letting the other players down?"

"Yes, you can do whatever you want, but will the decision put stress on your family?"

Yes might mean you are learning to state your opinion

"Yes, you can join the Hip Hop club, but you need to tell them what costume you like best."

"Yes, your teacher wants you to contrast the political positions, but he wants you to state your personal opinion."

"Yes, you can present your speech, but you need to tell your point of view."

"Yes, the teacher wants a summary, but she also wants you to explain the key points of the project."

"Yes, you can write about your experience, but don't forget to examine the strengths and weaknesses of the experience."

Yes might mean you are making new discoveries

"Yes, you can go on the trip, but you might want to add a few excursions to see the culture of the country."

"Yes, you are permitted to go to the conference, but you definitely want to attend the exhibit hall."

"Yes, the field trip is Friday, but you will want to explore the museum to see unusual artifacts."

"Yes, the exhibit is very rare, but you will want to talk with the tour guides about the unique exhibit on display."

"Yes, the display is vast, but you will want to pick a specific object to explore and write a brief description."

ಬ

Yes might mean you are building trust with others

"Yes, you can go with the church group, but be a good listener as some people may be struggling with issues."

"Yes, you can meet Judy, but be on time so she knows you are dependable."

"Yes, the group meets on Wednesdays, but respect each person's privacy as some people are sharing private information."

"Yes, he shared a very hurtful experience, so he needs your support right now."

"Yes, you can open up about losing your grandfather with your close friends."

ଔ

Yes might mean you are misleading others

"Yes, you can go to the prom, but be upfront with me about the cost of the dress, shoes and photos."

"Yes, you want to go to the game, but you need to be clear with me about the time of the game."

"Yes, you want to attend the birthday party, but did you provide me with the address of the party?"

"Yes, you can see your friends, but are you going to Mike's house or Bill's house?"

"Yes, the fair is tomorrow, but what time are you going to the fair?"

ଔ

Yes might mean there are suspicious circumstances

"Yes, you can go to the party, but I am a little suspicious that there is no invitation."

"Yes, the presentation is Thursday, but I'm a little suspicious that you have not practiced the presentation."

"Yes, the term paper is due tomorrow, but have you started typing it yet?"

"Yes, you have her phone number, but why does the number have a different area code?"

"Yes, final exams are next week, but have you started to review your notes and make a study guide?"

಄

Yes might mean you are losing credibility with others

"Yes, you can meet them, but it doesn't look very reliable if you are always late."

"Yes, you can go to the recreation center, but stop borrowing money from your friends."

"Yes, you have a group project, but did you finish the poster you were supposed to draw for the project?"

"Yes, you are mad at her, but you should not belittle her to your friends."

"Yes, you are smart, but you need to be responsible for completing your homework?"

03

Yes might mean you are isolating yourself from others

"Yes, you can go to the library, but stay near your friends."

"Yes, you can go to the park, but don't walk off by yourself."

"Yes, you can go to the mall, but don't go shopping by yourself, you need to stay with a friend."

"Yes, you can camp this weekend, by always stay with a buddy in the wilderness as a safety precaution."

"Yes, you can go to the concert, but stay with a group of friends as the stadium is big."

৪৩

CHAPTER EIGHT
Yes could mean implementing new ideas

Yes could mean that parents and adults are helping you to implement new ideas. This may include learning to reschedule tasks or interpreting something you are doing. Yes can also mean you are looking at alternatives or you have some gaps in your learning. Yes might also mean that you are lacking purpose in what you do and that you need to gain persistence in your path to success. Parents and teachers may be helping you to clarify ideas and implement your idea. Parents can help with reassurance of your plans and share information about opportunities to learn more things.

Yes might mean you need to reschedule tasks

"Yes, you can go to the gym, but reschedule the guitar lesson for Saturday."

"Yes, you can help with play rehearsal, but you need to call me 30 minutes before it ends so I can pick you up."

"Yes, you can go on the trip, but you need to schedule to leave after you take the placement test."

"Yes, you can go to the seminar, but you need to reschedule your orthodontic appointment."

"Yes, you are invited to the dance, but you need to reschedule your day for a hair appointment."

Yes might mean you need to interpret something

"Yes, you can take the course, but you need time to analyze the readings."

"Yes, you were assigned a project, but you need to write your interpretation of the results."

"Yes, the writings were different, but you need to interpret each writer's perspective and their personal angle of this important issue."

"Yes, the reading is interesting, but you need to interpret his unique style of writing."

"Yes, you can summarize the ideas, but you need to interpret her unusual point of view."

Yes might mean you need an alternative

"Yes, you can take the medical research track, but you can also take courses in medical careers."

"Yes, you can take two extracurricular activities, but you may need an alternative activity for winter break."

"Yes, you have to make a decision about the part-time job, but don't limit your alternatives."

"Yes, there are many choices, but look at the alternatives that most interest you."

"Yes, you want to go to an expensive college, but, look at some less expensive alternative colleges."

Yes might mean there are some gaps in your learning

"Yes, you researched the topic of measles, but did you consider both the doctor's and the patient's perspective?"

"Yes, your paper explores baseball, but did you discuss the careers related to the sport of baseball?"

"Yes, you sketched a neat drawing, but did you add any color to bring out some of the detail?"

"Yes, your math homework is complete, but did you show your work?"

"Yes, you reviewed some of the test topics, but did you complete a study guide for the test?"

Yes might mean you are lacking a purpose

"Yes, the paper has a lot of ideas, but what is the purpose of the paper?"

"Yes, the project has many details, but you need to narrow the focus so we know the purpose."

"Yes, the poster presentation is taking a lot of different directions, but the purpose should be clear to the audience."

"Yes, your speech contains a lot of information, but the audience needs to know your purpose."

"Yes, your portfolio contains so many artifacts, but you need to pick the artifacts related to the purpose of your portfolio."

ℬ

Yes might mean you need to gain persistence

"Yes, you are almost done with your term paper, but finish writing the summary."

"Yes, you have had the project half completed for weeks, but you need to put the final touches on the project."

"Yes, you have written your notes, but you need to develop the essay in an organized format."

"Yes, you were not selected for the dance team, but continue to audition because you have so much talent."

"Yes, you need to finish the project because it is a big part of your semester grade."

ଔ

Yes might mean you are clarifying your ideas

"Yes, you can go to the career fair, but complete the career interest form before you go."

"Yes, you mentioned your career goal is in the arts, but are you more interested in acting or directing?"

"Yes, there are part-time jobs at the fast food restaurant, but are you wanting a cook or cashier position?"

"Yes, you are interested in the business program, but your portfolio seems to be more focused on the art."

"Yes, we have internships, but you need to clarify which department you want to work in."

☙❧

Yes might mean you have to implement your ideas

"Yes, you can attend the summer camp, but you must submit a weeklong service project."

"Yes, the club officers will have to develop goals to implement for the school year."

"Yes, you have a great idea for the contest, but you need to get the team onboard so the ideas can be put into practice."

"Yes, you wrote the proposal, but you must decide the steps to implement your proposal ideas."

"Yes, you have a wonderful idea for a booth, but you need to assign the tasks to different people for the booth idea to be put into action."

☙

Yes might mean you need reassurance

"Yes, the presentation is tonight and I'm sure you will do a great job if you relax, smile and show your confidence."

"Yes, your speech sounds great, just relax and you will do fine."

"Yes, the interview is Thursday, so pick out your wardrobe, put a resume together and think about your strong points."

"Yes, the test is tomorrow, so go to bed early so you will be well rested for the test."

"Yes, the game is Friday and you have practiced everyday so you should be at your best."

✵

Yes might mean you have opportunities to learn new things

"Yes, you can attend the expo, but don't forget to pick up hand-outs from the exhibits."

"Yes, going on the trip would be a great way to see a new country."

"Yes, the camp will provide opportunities to see what a doctor's daily hospital rounds look like."

"Yes, the course provides opportunities to learn about engineering from hands on experiences and examples."

"Yes, the internship will help you decide which area of science you relate to and interests you the most."

CHAPTER NINE
Yes could mean life changes are happening

Parents and teachers could really be telling you 'yes' to prepare you for life changes. They might be helping you gain life readiness skills as you are gaining social maturity. This may be helping you to start self-monitoring and track your own personal progress. These adults want to observe as you emphasize the positive aspects of your life and gain a vision for the future. You will begin to goal set and then look at your outcomes. Most importantly you are learning to cope with change as you are making life transitions.

Yes might mean you are gaining life readiness skills

"Yes, now that you have completed the pre-requisites, you can choose your field of interest."

"Yes, your scholarship application looks complete and ready to be sent to college."

"Yes, you were very responsible putting together the reception and it shows in your organizational skills."

"Yes, the camp is two days away and I like the way you are already packed and ready to go."

"Yes, the application was received in time and thanks for checking to make sure all your paperwork was turned in."

ଚ

Yes might mean you are starting to self-monitor

"Yes, I liked the way you paced yourself in getting the huge project organized and completed on time."

"Yes, you pulled together all the props so they were in place for the show tonight."

"Yes, you were able to monitor the situation and stay calm even when the emotions were tense."

"Yes, your actions were appropriate for handling a large crowd of people."

"Yes, I like the way you empathized with the lady during the confrontation and you handled yourself well."

Yes might mean you are tracking your progress

"Yes, I like your tally sheet for recording the votes in the student election."

"Yes, you made a nice chart to show the progress in completing the projects."

"Yes, you can manage your progress by completing a checklist of the items that you need to turn in."

"Yes, you checked off all of the items required for the notebook check."

"Yes, I like the list you made of your upcoming assignments for each class."

☙

Yes might mean you are gaining social maturity

"Yes, I liked the way you introduced your friends to each other."

"Yes, you were calm even though he was yelling at you."

"Yes, you gave your teacher respect, when the other students were being immature and rude."

"Yes, you supported your friend even though he was frustrated about the grade."

"Yes, I liked the way you showed honor and respect to the principal as she retired after 30 years from the school."

Yes might mean you are emphasizing the positive aspects of your life

"Yes, you stepped up to the challenge of completing a big task in a short period of time."

"Yes, you have a challenging job, but you handle stress well."

"Yes, you are so calm as you run three machines at the same time."

"Yes, your energy level has remained high even though you have been incredibly busy your senior year."

"Yes, you turned a bad situation into a humorous experience for your friends and classmates."

Yes might mean having a vision for the future

"Yes, your interests keep leading you toward the area of dance."

"Yes, your skills in music are getting noticed by many colleges and universities as they spotted your talent in the competition."

"Yes, your knowledge of medical careers will help you in choosing a major in college."

"Yes, your sports' ranking will get you noticed by college recruiters."

"Yes, you have many strengths in the math area and that could help you in deciding which math program to choose."

ଔ

Yes might mean you are goal setting

"Yes, you are planning a busy summer with lots of personal goals."

"Yes, I like your goal to complete school a semester early since you took additional classes in the summer session."

"Yes, you have an interesting goal of making it into the state ping-pong championships your first year of training."

"Yes, the goal for the group is similar to your individual goals."

"Yes, your goal to make the state finals seems to be becoming a reality."

☙

Yes might mean you are looking at outcomes

"Yes, the outcome looks good for you to be recruited by a major college football team as coaches are already calling you."

"Yes, the outcome of your hard work is paying off as you could win a swimming scholarship."

"Yes, there could be some positive outcomes for making good grades in high school."

"Yes, the outcomes for hard work will be noticed by your boss and your supervisors."

"Yes, your teacher notices your effort in the beginning computer class so she is recommending you for the advanced class."

Yes might mean you are coping with change

"Yes, you are handling the injury well and have adjusted to your limitations."

"Yes, the move has been difficult, but you are adapting well to your new community."

"Yes, the change in your schedule is an inconvenience, but you are making it work by adjusting the pace you walk to class."

"Yes, the change to a new school is hard, but you are making new friends."

"Yes, the loss of a teacher is hard, but you seem to be handling the situation with a good attitude."

Yes might mean you are making many life transitions

"Yes, you finished your junior year and your senior year should be filled with fun activities."

"Yes, you are almost done with high school, so you can start planning for college."

"Yes, the senior project is complete so you can think about your next assignment."

"Yes, you passed your last exam so you meet the requirements and can prepare to graduate from high school."

"Yes, this is the last day of high school so say good bye to your many friends and hello to the future."

RECOMMENDED READING FOR TEENAGERS

Carlson, R. (2000). *Don't sweat the small stuff for teens: simple ways to keep cool in stressful times.* New York: Hyperion.

Covey, S. (1998). *The 7 habits of highly effective teens.* New York: Touchstone.

Espeland, P. (2003). *Life lists for teens.* Minneapolis: Free Spirit Publishing

Graham, S. (2000). *Teens can make it happen.* New York: Touchstone.

Shipp, Josh (2010). *The teen's guide to world domination: Advice on life, liberty and pursuit of awesomeness.* New York: St. Martin's Griffin.

INDEX

A

Actions, 7, 32
Adaptive, 53
Alternative, 81
Annoying, 25
Approval, 10
Attention, 27
Avoiding, 24
Awareness, 28

C

Change, 89, 98
Clarifying, 85
Collaborate, 63
Complaining, 29
Communication, 23
Complex, 62
Connections, 66
Consequences, 22
Conversation, 41
Coping, 98
Credibility, 76

D

Decision, 55
Details, 5
Differences, 64
Difficulties, 23
Disagreements, 58
Discoveries, 72
Disrupting, 32

E

Events, 69

Example, 37, 42

F

Feedback, 38
Feelings, 39
Focus, 18, 20
Future, 95

G

Gaps, 82
Goal setting, 96

H

Habits, 51
Health, 68

I

Ideas, 78, 85, 86
Information, 13
Implement, 86
Interests, 44
Interpret, 80
Introductions, 35
Involvement, 19
Isolating, 77

L

Learning, 82
Learning cycle, 56
Life, 62, 89, 90, 94, 99
Listen, 31
Limitations, 49

M

Misleading, 74
Mistake, 40
Modify, 11

O
Observations, 60
One-sided, 26
Opinion, 71
Opportunities, 88
Others, 67, 76, 77
Outcomes, 97
Outside, 76

P
Persistence, 84
Personal decision, 55
Picture, 12
Plans, 17
Practical approach, 54
Problem solve, 65
Progress, 92
Purpose, 83

Q
Questions, 1, 3

R
Reassurance, 87
Readiness, 90
Realistic view, 61
Reconsidered, 2
Re-Evaluate, 8
Reconvene, 9
Relations, 67
Reschedule, 79
Retrace, 21
Review, 6
Routine, 57

S
Self-monitoring, 91
Setback, 17
Situation, 15, 59
Social interaction, 34
Social maturity, 93
Support, 36
Supportive environment, 52
Steps, 16, 21
Story, 14
Strengths, 48
Suspicious, 75

T
Talent, 43
Tasks, 79
Transition, 45, 46, 99
Tracking, 92
Trouble spots, 50
Trust, 73

U
Unclear, 33
Upset, 30

V
Value, 64
View, 61

W
Weaknesses, 47

Y
Yourself, 70

www.ingramcontent.com/pod-product-compliance
Lightning Source LLC
Chambersburg PA
CBHW030331080526
44584CB00012B/814

*9 7 8 1 9 4 0 1 3 6 0 0 4 *